Linear B

and related scripts

Cover pic The
difference urnt;
the darke

Pylos tablet An 1, list of rowers who are to go to Pleuron.

Linear B
and related scripts

John Chadwick

University of California Press/British Museum

Acknowledgments

I should like to thank my friend and colleague, Dr J. T. Killen for reading and criticising the text of this book. The views expressed are entirely my own responsibility.

I am indebted for photographs to the Department of Classics of the University of Cincinnati, USA (figs. 2, 5, 17, 23) and for the cover picture by Alison Frantz. I should like also to thank the École française d' Archéologie of Athens for fig. 37, and the Cabinet des Médailles, Bibliothèque Nationale of Paris for fig. 35.

The line drawings have been based with their permission on the originals by E. L. Bennett, Jr, J-P. Olivier, L. Godart. E. Masson and O. Masson. I am grateful to all of these for their interest and help. Fig. 22 is reproduced from A. J. Evans, *Scripta Minoa* I, p. 156, Clarendon Press, Oxford, 1909, by permission of the publisher.

University of California Press
Berkeley and Los Angeles California

© 1987 The Trustees of the British Museum

Designed by Arthur Lockwood
Front cover design by Grahame Dudley

Printed in Great Britain

Volume 1 in the *Reading the Past* series

Library of Congress Cataloging-in-Publication Data

Chadwick, John, 1920–
  Linear B and related scripts.
  (Reading the past)
  Bibliography: p.
  Includes index.
  1. Inscriptions, Linear B.   2. Inscriptions, Linear A.
3. Inscriptions, Cypro-Minoan.   4. Phaistos Disk.
I. Title.   II. Series.
P1035.C54   1987   481'.7   86-19205
ISBN 0-520-06019-9 (alk. paper)

Contents

1
The Discovery
of Linear B

The revelation of the Bronze Age in the Aegean area began with the epoch-making discoveries of Heinrich Schliemann at Troy and Mycenae towards the end of the nineteenth century. At that date the science of archaeology had hardly come into existence, and we ought not to blame Schliemann for the irreparable damage that he did to the sites he attacked. At Troy he dug a great cutting through the middle of the hill to expose the earliest layers. But at least he demonstrated that there had been civilisations in the Aegean long before the historical Greeks came on the scene, even though we now know that what he originally identified as Priam's Troy was in fact a thousand years too early for the Trojan War of Greek tradition.

Now that the chronology has been well established, we can confidently assert that the greatest pre-classical civilisation flourished in what is called, after the first of its sites to be excavated, the Mycenaean period. This can be dated roughly between the sixteenth and twelfth centuries BC. It is generally believed that the epics of Homer describe the Aegean world towards the end of that period; but the more facts we learn about it, the more it is evident that Homer's knowledge was incomplete and imperfect. We have moved a long way from Schliemann's faith in the literal truth of Homer.

An English student of archaeology, Arthur Evans (later Sir Arthur), was so impressed by the level of culture these Mycenaeans had achieved on the mainland of Greece, that he formed the opinion that such a civilisation could not have functioned without a knowledge of writing. Yet neither at Troy nor at Mycenae had Schliemann's excavations yielded a single inscription. Whether Evans' opinion was justified may be disputed, but his hunch proved to be right, and it was he who succeeded in finding the proof, though it led to such important new discoveries that he later lost interest in the problem that had started his search.

He noted that dealers in antiquities in Athens sometimes had engraved stones for sale, which had clearly been intended for use as seals. They were unlike any later seals, and were covered with small pictures of objects arranged in such a way that they might be a system of writing. It may be hard in such cases to be sure whether the signs are really writing, or merely a pictorial representation of a name. Heraldic shields, for instance, often have devices which suggest the owner's name. But Evans thought the system on these seal-stones was more like a script, and his researches led him to the conclusion that they had come from the great island of Crete.

At this date Crete was still occupied by the Turks, and successive Greek revolts throughout the nineteenth century were unsuccessful until 1899, when the Turks finally withdrew. Evans had already travelled widely through the island, and had decided where to dig. The site he chose was Knossos, a few miles inland from the principal town of the island, now known as Iraklion. Greek traditions told of a King Minos who had in prehistoric times ruled a sea-empire in the Aegean from Knossos. It seemed therefore a promising site to investigate, and local diggers had already recovered interesting finds from it. When the Turks left, Evans was able to purchase it, and he began digging there in 1900.

1   Knossos tablet Co 907, listing sheep, goats, pigs and cattle

It became clear at once that he had found a major Bronze Age site, and he was rewarded by the discovery of large numbers of inscribed clay tablets. The writing was much more highly-developed than on the seal-stones, and there could be no doubt that this was a true script. But the characters were unlike any script then known, and although Evans started with high hopes of deciphering it, his work came fairly soon to an end, for it was overshadowed by more exciting finds.

Evans had hoped to find a Mycenaean site on Crete to rival Mycenae on the mainland. Sure enough, the huge complex of buildings he unearthed at Knossos must have been a major palace, and it had flourished during the Mycenaean period. But it differed in type from the site at Mycenae, and what was quite unexpected was that it went back much further in time. The king of Knossos was living in some degree of luxury long before the walls of Mycenae were built. In fact, it is now accepted that a high level of civilisation developed in Crete as much as two hundred years before the mainland began to imitate it. It was no longer possible to call this Mycenaean, and Evans coined the new term 'Minoan' to describe the Bronze Age culture of Crete.

Many archaeologists followed Evans to Crete, and important new palaces were excavated at Phaistos in the south and Mallia further to the east along the north coast. Both of these sites and several others, notably Haghia Triada only a few miles from Phaistos, produced small quantities of clay tablets, but these were rather different from the Knossos ones. Evans thought at first this might be due to a special royal script at Knossos, but later it was seen that the differences correlated with the date. The earliest inscriptions were those on the seal-stones, rarely found on clay; Evans named this script 'hieroglyphic' because of a supposed resemblance to the early Egyptian script known by that name, but there is no reason to think that they are related. A little later the pictures of objects become more stylised and thus less recognisable, especially when written on clay. Evans named this script Linear A, because the signs were simple outlines. Few examples of this were found at Knossos, for there the bulk of the inscriptions were in a later version of this script, which he called Linear B. This was restricted to the latest phase of the Palace, which we can now date as from about 1450–1375 BC.

The clay tablets had not been baked when they were made, but only dried in the sun, so that they survived only if they happened to be in a building which had been burnt. Thus tablets were only found in destruction layers, and must date to the very end of the period of the building's use. Unfortunately, at Knossos there has been since Evans' time a long argument over the date of the final destruction, and although most scholars accept a date somewhere around 1375 BC, it has been seriously proposed that a date in the thirteenth century would be possible. There is nothing in the documents to settle the argument, but on the whole a fourteenth century date still seems more likely.

Evans studied his Linear B tablets and drew some obvious conclusions. But although he prepared an edition of all the hieroglyphic material then known, his preparations for an edition of the Linear B tablets were still incomplete when the outbreak of the Balkan Wars, and then the First World War, diverted his attention to other matters. After the war he produced his vast work on the palace at Knossos, which he confidently named the Palace of Minos. This contained a section on the tablets, and a number of them were illustrated, but the vast bulk of the documents still remained unpublished and hence inaccessible to scholars. It was not until 1952, eleven years after Evans' death, that an old friend and colleague, Sir John Myres, finally published the volume that Evans had planned and largely compiled around 1911–12.

It was unfortunate in many ways that it had been so long delayed. Earlier publication would have made a great deal of information available, so that serious work on the decipherment could have started much earlier; even those who succeeded in seeing material in Iraklion Museum were inhibited by the rule that no one may anticipate in print the finder's first publication of his finds. When it became possible for scholars to work on the originals, it was quickly discovered that the edition had been imperfect and incomplete. Three separate collections of fragments of tablets recovered in Evans' excavations have since come to light in

Iraklion Museum, but none of these appear in the 1952 publication. Their study at once revealed that no serious effort had been made to join the fragments, and so to reconstruct complete, or more nearly complete, tablets. This task has fallen to a devoted band of scholars of several different nationalities, who have worked together as a team to reconstitute the tablets and publish a complete and trustworthy text.

But as early as 1939 a major new discovery had totally changed the situation as regards Linear B. In that year a joint American–Greek expedition under Carl W. Blegen of the University of Cincinnati had begun to excavate a site in the south–west of the Greek mainland. It lies a little to the north of the modern town of Pylos, just inland from the Bay of Navarino, one of the finest natural harbours in the Mediterranean. It proved to be a Mycenaean palace destroyed by fire at the end of the thirteenth century BC. By a stroke of luck the first trench laid out by the excavators ran across what we now know as the Archive Room, since it contained hundreds of clay tablets, hardened by the fire which destroyed it. As soon as the first pieces were lifted from the ground, they could be identified as written in the same Linear B script already well known from Knossos.

This news did not perhaps create the sensation it should have done. The world had more serious matters on its mind in 1939–40 than Bronze Age writing. For the

2   Pylos tablet Tn 996, showing numbers of bath-tubs and other vessels, some of bronze, some gold

first time Linear B was seen to be not restricted to Knossos, or even to Crete, but to be in use on the mainland, for such an archive is hardly likely to have been transported from where it was written. Yet if it were simply, as Evans asserted, a modified version of Linear A, a purely Cretan script, did this mean that the Cretan language too was used on the Greek mainland? Was this the proof Evans had sought to show that all southern Greece had once been under Minoan control?

The difficulty was that most scholars at this time believed that the Mycenaeans known to archaeology were the Achaeans described by Homer as masters of Greece at the time of the Trojan War. Of course poets, like novelists, are liable to make their characters speak their own language; but the fact that most of Homer's characters have names which are significant in Greek implied that Greek was already spoken in Greece in the Mycenaean age, if Homer's stories were not pure fiction. So what was the king of Mycenaean Pylos, Nestor, if we can trust Homer, doing keeping his accounts in a foreign language?

An easy answer to this question is provided by the parallel of the Middle Ages, when kings all over Europe kept their records in Latin, whatever language they spoke themselves. However, further discoveries from other sites on the mainland have now totally altered the picture. Linear B is now seen to be the script of the Mycenaean palaces on the mainland, and it is its intrusion into Crete which is the feature which demands explanation. The solution to the problem came in 1952–3, with the demonstration that the language of the Linear B tablets was Greek. Evans would have been profoundly shocked to learn that his Minoan palace in the last phase of its existence had used the Greek language. This story will form the subject of the next chapter, but we need first to complete the account of discovery.

Even before Linear B tablets had been found on the mainland, it was known that large pottery jars with painted inscriptions in this script had been found on the mainland. The largest collection is from Thebes, to the north-west of Athens, but other contemporary sites have provided specimens. These jars were often used for the transport of olive oil and wine, and it was suggested that these were containers for Cretan produce. This suggestion has now been confirmed in a remarkable way. It was noticed that some of the words on the jars were also found on the Knossos Linear B tablets, where they appeared to be place names; and it would be natural for the exporter to record his name and address on his product. But much more recently an analysis of the clay used to make these jars has revealed that they almost certainly come from Crete.

Small numbers of clay tablets have been found at Mycenae itself, the first significant find being made by the British archaeologist A. J. B. Wace in 1952. He dug some large houses outside the Citadel Walls, and found in them collections of Linear B tablets. This does not prove that Linear B was in widespread use throughout the population, for such houses must have been occupied by members of the royal establishment. Some more, rather badly damaged tablets, have come from a house within the walls, but there is no trace of the main palace archive. Since the palace is at the top of the hill, its site has long been exposed to the weather, and its archives are likely to have perished. But it is a sobering thought that if Schliemann had known what to look for, he might have been the first to find Linear B tablets. As they come out of the ground, it is only too easy to dismiss fragments of tablets as pieces of coarse pottery, which the early excavators threw away without a thought.

At Tiryns, only a few miles away from Mycenae, stood a huge castle with massive walls. It may have been intended to guard the port, but the sea has now retreated from the site. It would be incredible if this were, as Homer implies, the seat of an independent kingdom. It must have been in some sense under the control of the king of Mycenae, who may have been an overlord having the allegiance of several lesser rulers. From 1971 onwards excavations in the lower town outside the castle walls have revealed a number of fragmentary Linear B tablets. It looks as if these have come down from their original position higher up, and all we can say at the moment is that somewhere on this site there must have been a major archive, but only fragments of it have been recovered.

The situation at Thebes is rather different. The problem here is that the same site has been continuously occupied for at least four thousand years, and it is now a thriving provincial town. This has been built over successive layers of occupation, Turkish, Frankish, Byzantine, Roman, Hellenistic, Classical, Archaic, Mycenaean and even earlier. It is rarely possible here to find a place to excavate, and only when it is necessary to put up a new building are the archaeologists able to investigate what lies beneath the ground. Rescue digs of this kind have so far yielded two small collections of Linear B tablets, and a group of clay sealings, small lumps of clay stamped with a seal and then in some cases inscribed with a few words in Linear B. This evidence makes it almost certain that somewhere below the centre of the modern town lies an archive of tablets. Thebes was clearly the site of a palace which controlled a large kingdom in this part of Greece, and its records would be very important, if we could only find them. But for the moment we can say very little about this kingdom.

The finds show that writing was not in widespread use in Mycenaean Greece. No tablets have been found at minor sites, and all those where they have been found are either palaces or so close to palaces that they can be regarded as dependencies. There is no trace of any private use of writing. This contrasts with the history of the Greek alphabet, which as early as the eighth century BC was used by private citizens to write light-hearted verses on a cup; and during the next two centuries began to be used for laws inscribed on stone in places where all could read them. Nothing of the kind has ever been found in Linear B. Writing seems to have been exclusively a bureaucratic tool, a necessary method of keeping administrative accounts and documents, but never used for historical or even frivolous purposes. As we shall see, the contents of Linear B tablets are almost without exception lists of people, animals, agricultural produce and manufactured objects. But first we must see how it became possible to read a script which had been forgotten for more than three thousand years.

2
The Decipherment

The first step in trying to decipher an unknown script is the analysis of the texts. We need to know what sort of a script it is, and what can be deduced about the contents of the inscriptions. All scripts can be classified as one of three types: *a*) phonetic, *b*) ideographic, *c*) mixed. Phonetic scripts represent by their signs the sounds of the language. They do not of course give a detailed picture of those sounds; for one thing, it would be confusing if every speaker wrote exactly as he spoke, for then the same utterance would be recorded in many different ways. There is therefore a conventional element in scripts which eliminates most of the individual differences between speakers. Secondly, to represent even roughly the range of sounds employed would demand a much larger alphabet that the twenty-six letters we use in English; many languages employ diacritical marks on letters to indicate special values, but even so all phonetic scripts are only a notation adequate to permit someone who knows the language to reconstruct the word for himself. The segments into which the stream of speech is analysed for notation may vary in size. Alphabetic scripts aim at the ideal of one sign for each sound, though English, for example, often departs from this ideal. Other languages in the past have used syllabic scripts, where each sign represents a pronounceable syllable. These may vary from the simple type where each sign denotes a consonant followed by a vowel, to more complex types where there are signs for vowels followed by consonants, and for groups of consonant, vowel and consonant, and so on.

Ideographic scripts have basically one sign for each word, and this sign usually represents the meaning of the word, not primarily its phonetic form. They can therefore be easily transferred from one language to another. So the Japanese borrowed the Chinese ideographic script, and wrote the same signs for the same meanings, but gave them quite different sounds. The problem with ideographic scripts is that they need enormous numbers of signs, which have to be very complex in order to be different, and are therefore hard to learn and to write. However, the advantage for the decipherer is that they are easily recognisable by the large number of different signs and their complexity. Ideograms usually begin as pictures of objects, and they may despite development still remain recognisable, but they may also evolve to unrecognisable patterns, the meaning of which is simply conventional. A familiar set of ideograms, the numerals *1, 2, 3, 4, 5*, can be read in English as *one, two, three, four, five*, but the same signs may be used in other languages with quite different phonetic values, although their meaning remains the same.

Mixed systems are not uncommon, that is, ones where some signs are ideographic and some phonetic. When we read *1st* as *first*, and *3rd* as *third*, we are using ideograms with a phonetic complement. This serves to prevent us giving the wrong sound to the ideogram, and in some languages allows us to indicate inflected forms. Examples of mixed scripts are Hittite (a cuneiform script) in antiquity, and in modern times, Japanese.

This explanation is essential in order to understand how Linear B was deciphered. It was immediately obvious that there was a simple numeral system; virtually all tablets record numerals, and there are examples of addition to verify the system. There are signs for units (short upright bars), tens (horizontal bars), hundreds (circles) and thousands (circles with rays). Each sign can be repeated up to nine times. Thus the number 1357 would be written:

With this clue it is then possible to identify certain signs which occur only in isolation before numerals. Many of these are obvious pictures, or 'pictograms' as they are called:

But many others bear only a distant relationship to the pictures that must underlie them, and at this stage these are therefore still unidentified. Even so it is clear that some of these were animals:

There is also a special set of signs which occur before numerals and sometimes following an ideogram. The analysis of a Knossos tablet will illustrate this.

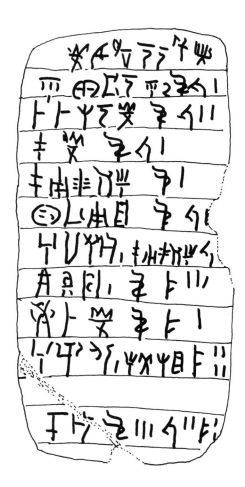

3   Knossos tablet Fp1

Now if we call $\maltese$ *A* and the signs $\maltese$ and $\maltese$ *x* and *y* respectively, we can tabulate the entries thus:

A	x	y
0	1	–
0	2	–
0	1	–
1	–	–
0	1?	–
0	1?	–
0	0	3
0	0	1
0	0	4
3	2	2

The last line is a much higher figure than any of the preceding ones, and this would be explained if it were a total. But since this is a sum like our old-fashioned pounds, shillings and pence, we need to know the relationship between the three columns to check this, because it will be necessary to carry over the appropriate figure from one column to that to the left of it. If we add up the figures in the right-hand column, they come to 8; but the total in the last line is only 2. It follows therefore that $x = 6y$ or $3y$, either of which would give the remainder 2, if divided into 8. But since one entry has the figure $4y$, if $x = 3y$, this would have been written $1x$ $1y$. Therefore $x = 6y$, and 1 must be added to the middle column.

The figures in the middle column add up to 6, to which must be added the 1 carried over from the y column. But two of the figures are shown as $1?$, because either or both of these could be read as 2. However, when the total of x is reduced to A units, there is again a remainder of 2, as shown by the total. Since only $1A$ is recorded in the left-hand column, 2 must be carried over from the x column to make the total $3A$. It follows that the total of x units, before being reduced to the higher unit A, must be an even number, if when divided by twice the value of x it leaves a remainder of 2. Therefore only one of the doubtful figures must be restored as 2, and the other is 1. Thus the real total for the x column will be 8, and therefore $A = 3x = 18y$. By such means we can establish that the word 𐀞 𐀡 (and elsewhere 𐀞 𐀢) is used to introduce a total, and must have an appropriate meaning.

Inspection of other tablets shows that x and y are fractions of other ideograms too, and thus we can can deduce that they are units of a system of measurement, like hundredweights, quarters, pounds and ounces, or bushels, gallons, quarts and pints. Thus the numerals lead directly to the identification of three series of metric signs: one, since its highest unit is a pictogram of a pair of scales, is clearly weights; the other two share the two lowest units, so they presumably represent volume, one for dry and the other for liquid measure.

By such deductions it is easy to see that the tablets are for the most part lists of men and women, livestock, agricultural produce and manufactured objects. Without any knowledge of the language, we can still give a useful account of the subject matter of the records. As we shall see later, this is also the situation as regards the earlier, Linear A, script.

The real problem concerns the remaining signs, which constitute the bulk of the text. The first question to ask is: how many are there? This is not so easy to answer as might be thought. The scribes did not write a 'copy-book' hand, but showed a great deal of individual variation. One sign appears as:

These are fairly obviously variants of one sign. But another, rather similar sign, appears as:

Is the number of strokes inside the circle significant, or are they all simply variants? Is it the same as the previous sign? The answers to these questions depend partly on judgment, but a hunch can often be confirmed if two forms behave alike and replace each other in the same sign group. Simple as this sounds, it does of course depend upon having a large body of material to work on. Statistical methods cannot be used when there are very few examples of a particular sign. For fifty years after the first discovery of Linear B, very few people had access to enough material to make this kind of work practicable. Evans produced some lists of signs based upon the Knossos tablets; but it was impossible to check his work, and when the fuller evidence was published in 1952, the job had already been done for the Pylos tablets by an American, Emmett L. Bennett. His signary still stands today, with minor modifications, as the definitive list of signs. But there are still a very few signs whose status is unclear. For instance, Bennett quite properly listed as separate signs ⲫ and 𝆏, although this would be the only case in the script in which the distinction between two signs depended on one being the mirror image of the other. Subsequently it has become clear that these were really variants of one sign, since new material has shown that one replaced the other in the same sign-group. Bennett in his table listed 87 signs, and even with corrections it is safe to say the total number in use was no more than 90.

Once the signary was established, it became possible to count the signs and list their frequencies. It is highly convenient for the decipherer that the Mycenaean scribes divided their signs into groups by using a short upright bar placed just above the line, thus:

$$ 𝕋𝓜\ 🝔𝝠𝕭.\ ⊕𝝒𝟤.𝕔𝕓\ 𝓜𝕭.\ 𝓐𝝔𝄆 $$

The groups so divided off range from two to eight signs. Contrast this with the habit of Greek alphabetic inscriptions, which usually string the words together in a continuous sequence.

The direction of the writing is obvious, since most lines begin at the left-hand edge of the tablet and unfilled spaces are left at the right-hand edge. This left-to-right direction is uniform throughout Linear B. Tablets with several lines of writing usually have them separated by transverse lines running the full width of the tablet. It is tempting to call them rules, but they are in fact drawn by hand, before the text was written. Elongated tablets often have the first word of the text in large signs, and after this there is a division into two lines. In places a word, or even a complete line of writing, is added over the text; this is either an annotation, or may be a continuation of the main text for which there was not enough room.

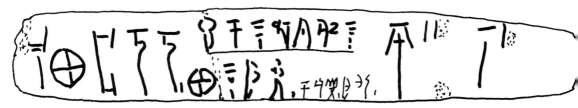

4   Pylos tablet Eo 269, showing division into two lines

The tablets are generally speaking small enough to be held in one hand, while being written on by the other; they sometimes have the marks of fingers on the reverse. The largest tablet so far known is about six inches across, ten-and-a-half inches high, and about an inch thick, but the majority are very much smaller.

Thus it is possible to produce frequency lists of signs, showing not only their overall frequency, but also in initial, medial and final positions. It will often appear that a sign has a particular liking for one position in sign-groups. At this stage it is useful to compile an index of sign-groups, not merely to find repetitions of groups, but also to discover groups which begin alike but have different endings. Likewise a reverse index, that is to say, one in which the groups are arranged in the order of their signs working from the end of the word, is useful to find groups that have the same ending.

All of this work was performed for Linear B by the small number of people who had access to sufficient texts, but it did not at first lead to any significant advances. The most important step, seen with hindsight, was the discovery by the American scholar Alice Kober of a number of sign-groups at Knossos which occurred in three different forms, which she thought must represent some sort of inflexional endings.

The decipherment proper was the work of a British amateur named Michael Ventris. He had been fascinated by the mystery of Linear B since he was a schoolboy, and when he had qualified as an architect, he continued to devote much of his spare time to this hobby. In the autumn of 1951 the publication of the first batch of Pylos tablets, those found in 1939, gave him for the first time an adequate supply of material. He had already analysed the script and concluded that in view of the size of the signary it was likely to be a relatively simple syllabic system. He also understood the ideographic system, as outlined above.

If the language of the inscriptions had been known, it should not have proved too difficult to find values which would give appropriate words. However, as explained above, Linear B was seen as a Cretan script, which had unexpectedly appeared on the mainland of Greece in a Mycenaean palace. Evans had been in no doubt that his 'Minoan' Cretans were not Greek-speakers, and it could be held that the Pylos tablets supported his belief that the Minoans had for a time controlled southern Greece, as they certainly did the islands of the Aegean. Other scholars were less certain, for Homer gives what is acknowledged to be a picture of the Mycenaean age, however much the details are garbled. All his characters speak Greek, whether they are on the Greek or Trojan side; and many have names which are significant in Greek, and this too is true of the Trojans. But this could be simply a literary convention, and it is unsafe to deduce from Homer's poems that the Mycenaean inhabitants of Greece were Greek-speaking, though this certainly appeared for other reasons too to be probable. The upshot was that it was clearly impossible to predict the language of Linear B, and Greek would have been regarded as an outsider if this had been a betting matter.

There was however another valuable clue. At the easternmost fringe of the early Greek world lay the island of Cyprus, which was largely Greek-speaking in classical times, though early inscriptions in other languages showed that it had not always been wholly Greek. Down to about the third century BC the Greeks of Cyprus had not used the alphabet, but a peculiar script of their own. This had been deciphered in the 1870s, since it was assumed to be Greek, and few short inscriptions were known in which the same text was given both in the later Greek alphabet and in the native script. Fuller details will be given in chapter 6, but it was important that here was a simple syllabic script used for writing Greek. Even more interesting was the fact that a few of the simple signs were identical with or very similar to signs in Linear B. Evans had already noticed that a Knossos tablet listing horses contained the word ⊐† and that ʃ† in the Cypriot script would read *po-lo*. Now *pōlos* is the Greek word for 'foal'. Evans dismissed this as a coincidence, and in principle he was right to do so. For one thing the word is very short; a coincidence involving a longer word would be less easy to dismiss. To prove that Linear B was Greek would require a number of such coincidences, where the meaning of the word could already be deduced from the context. Evans was of course in any case irrevocably prejudiced against the Greek solution.

Ventris started by deliberately ignoring the Cypriot clue as the point of departure. Observing that the formula for 'total' varied between ∓⅄ and ∓⅄, he argued that in an inflected language this might correspond to a difference of gender, since one form appears with the ideogram for 'man', the other with the ideogram for 'woman'. If the gender difference was expressed by a change in the vowel of the termination, then ⅄ and ⅄ probably differed in their vowels, but had the same consonant. Detailed analysis of a number of such pairs of words enabled Ventris to build a 'grid', a table in which the signs sharing the same consonant were arranged in horizontal lines, and those sharing the same vowel in vertical columns. Once this stage had been reached for a fair number of signs, it was only necessary to obtain values for a few of the signs and it would become possible to read off the values of the rest.

At this point the Cypriot clue afforded some help, but the key discovery concerned the groups noticed by Alice Kober. Ventris, seeing that they did not occur on the Pylos tablets, deduced that they might be the names of Cretan towns, with their adjectival variants; and since the names familiar from classical Crete are not of Greek origin, it was not unreasonable to suppose that they came from the earlier language of Crete. He was quickly able to suggest that *ko-no-so* was a spelling for what in Greek is *Knōsos*, *a-mi-ni-so* was the name of its port, *Amnisos*, and a few other well-known names were identified. Up to this point the decipherment was still not linked to any language. But application of the values so obtained from the 'grid' to other words revealed that, for instance, the totalling formula would read *to-so* and *to-sa*, which bore a striking resemblance to the Greek word meaning 'so much' or 'so many', *tosos*, feminine *tosā*. A few other words also appeared which recalled Greek words of appropriate meaning.

Ventris therefore set out to test the hypothesis that the language was Greek, not expecting it to lead anywhere. But as he applied his values to more and more words,

Greek words kept on appearing, but their spelling was nearly always incomplete, and the written skeleton needed to be filled out before it became intelligible as a Greek word. Even so, the form of the word was sometimes unfamiliar, as might be expected in a form of Greek far older than our earliest text, the poems of Homer.

For example, there were tablets from Pylos listing numbers of women, clearly recognisable from the ideogram, together with numbers of two other items written in the syllabic script. It was a fair assumption that these were the words for 'children', or more precisely 'girls' and 'boys'. Homeric Greek has for these the words *kourai* and *kouroi*, but the Linear B spellings emerged as *ko-wa* and *ko-wo*.

5   Pylos tablet Aa 62, showing women and children

Only a knowledge of the etymology and early history of Greek could show that the original form of these words had been *korwai* and *korwoi*. The letter pronounced *w* had been lost from Homeric Greek, though it was still heard in a few dialects. But it was necessary to set up rules stating that *r* might be omitted before *w*, and that diphthongs might have their second element dropped, so that the ending might be read as -*ai* and -*oi*.

It was at this point that Ventris formed an alliance with John Chadwick, a lecturer in Classics at Cambridge University, whose special interest was the early history of the Greek language. Together they worked out the rules governing the spelling, which will be discussed more fully in the next chapter; they were able to show that in many cases the archaic form of the words they reconstructed was supported by what was already known about the language.

The increasing number of Greek words which appeared in promising contexts soon provided good evidence for the correctness of the decipherment. For instance, previous decipherments had sometimes yielded weird names, which their authors claimed as gods and goddesses; the Ventris decipherment applied to a Knossos tablet yielded no less than four divine names well known from Greek literature. But it was necessary to present these results in a scientific manner, so that any scholar with the skill and patience to apply the solution could see for himself the match between the interpreted forms and their contexts. Even where the context was itself obscure, the interpretation often produced a plausible sequence of Greek words.

All this was demonstrated in an article entitled 'Evidence for Greek dialect in the Mycenaean archives', written jointly by Ventris and Chadwick and published in *The Journal of Hellenic Studies* for 1953. The theory was so unexpected, and its testing demanded so much technical and archaeological knowledge, that its reception was at first mixed. But powerful support soon came from distinguished Greek scholars, and others began to contribute to the elucidation of the texts.

But the main reason why the decipherment carried conviction was an unforeseen event. In the summer of 1952, almost precisely at the critical period when Ventris was getting the first hint of Greek words, the American excavators of Pylos, whose work had been interrupted in 1939 by the outbreak of the Second World War, at last resumed digging. More Linear B tablets were quickly found, but as they came out of the ground they could not easily be read, and they were carefully stored for cleaning and consolidation during the ensuing winter. In the spring of 1953 the leader of the American team, Carl Blegen, returned to Greece to work on his finds. He had been supplied with an advance copy of the article reporting the decipherment, which was still being printed. Studying his new tablets Blegen quickly noticed a large one which bore pictures of three-legged cauldrons. He applied the values given to the accompanying signs, and was astonished to read *ti-ri-po-de*, almost exactly the Greek word *tripodes*, which of course means 'tripods' and is used of cauldrons of this type.

Even more remarkable was a series of vessels pictured on the same tablet with different numbers of loops at the top, clearly indicating the number of handles. Here the text revealed a word which read *qe-to-ro-we* accompanying the vessels with four handles, and one reading *ti-ri-o-we-e* or *ti-ri-jo-we* with those with three handles. Obviously the second word began again with *tri-*, the Greek form for the number 'three' in compounds; and those who knew about the history of the language could accept that *quetro-* was a possible form in very early Greek for 'four'. The classical form corresponding to this would be *tetra-*. There was even a pictogram of a vessel without handles; here the text read *a-no-we*, and Greek regularly has *an-* as a negative prefix. The second part of these words is related to the word for 'ear', which is also used in Greek to mean 'handle'.

As soon as the 'tripod' tablet became known, most scholars accepted the validity of the decipherment. The odds against a coincidence of this sort would be astronomical. In other tablets too, new examples were found of ideograms

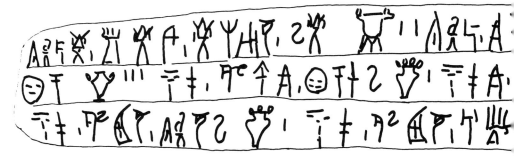

6   Pylos tablet Ta 641, showing tripod-cauldrons

corresponding to the syllabic text. The Knossos tablet listing horses has already been mentioned; a new fragment joined to this gave the Greek words for 'horses' in one line and 'asses' in the other. Added to the word for 'foals' already suggested, but rejected, by Evans, this made three words on one tablet in close agreement with the evident subject.

This did not mean that all was now plain sailing. A number of the rarer signs remained to be solved, and there are still a few left in this class. Some signs appeared to have an optional function, and the limits within which they could be used had to be determined. The nature of the spelling rules had to be elucidated, and the new dialect revealed had to be studied. The vocabulary proved, not surprisingly, to differ from that current a thousand years later, and only gradually has it become possible to suggest meanings for some of the new words.

Some of the early difficulties turned out to be due to wrong readings of the originals, and a great deal of effort has gone into their study. As a result we have much better texts now than were available to the decipherers. In particular, the joining of fragments in the material from Knossos has revealed many new facts. It is pleasant to record that all this work has been performed by the co-operation of scholars all over the world.

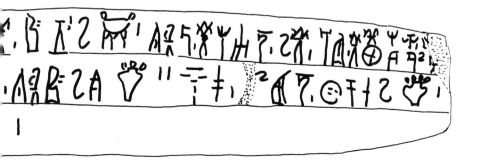

3
How the Linear B
Script was used

The Linear B script is now fairly well known and understood, though there are still many unsolved problems. It consists of three elements: syllabic signs, ideograms and numerals. The syllabic signs are used to spell out the phonetic shape of the word. The ideograms were not used as a means of writing a word, but merely as symbols to indicate what the numerals were counting. This means that ideograms are normally found only before numerals. In some cases the word describing the object being counted is first spelled out syllabically, and then the relevant ideogram is written before the numeral. The metric signs form a special class of ideograms, and these often occur after an ideogram specifying the commodity which is being measured.

As now known in the light of the decipherment, the Linear B syllabary consists of 87 signs. These may be divided into three classes, shown in the following tables.

The first of these (fig. 7) is the basic syllabary, which consists of signs for the five vowels, and signs for each of the twelve consonants combined with each of these vowels. Gaps in the table may indicate that there never existed a sign for that value, but one or two may be absent because they are still unidentified.

The forms shown are merely typical specimens, and there are a number of variant forms in use. Since we are dealing with handwriting, it is impossible to illustrate here all the varieties that may be encountered. There are some differences to be observed between the forms used at Knossos and on the mainland; but generally speaking the range of variation found at one site is as great as between different sites.

There is also a supplementary group of signs (fig. 8), which are in some sense optional. They are not strictly necessary, but may be employed to give a more accurate spelling and so reduce the risk of misinterpretation; or they may serve as abbreviations, allowing one sign to do the work of two. Their use will be explained further below. Some of the values are marked as uncertain; this is because we do not yet have enough examples in recognisable words for the value to be regarded as certainly determined. It is probable that the unidentified signs (fig. 9) belong mainly to this optional class.

The values shown must not be taken as a strict representation of the sounds; they are merely conventional notations, and interpretation is needed to reconstruct from them the spoken form. All scripts are in some sense merely an outline notation which the reader has to fill in for himself, and there are words in English which we need to recognise before we can read them correctly. But the Linear B spelling is far more incomplete, and the Mycenaean reader must have been left with a lot of guesswork in order to make intelligible words out of what he read on the tablet. This would be quite intolerable if the script were used as we understand writing; it would be very difficult to use it for letters or histories. But in fact, with one exception, it seems to have been used solely for writing lists and accounts; and these too were hardly intended to be read by anyone but the writer and his colleagues working in the same office. The one exception is the inscribed jars, which seem to record the name, and sometimes other details, of the producer of the contents. In these circumstances a much more abbreviated script may be acceptable. But for us, trying to read these texts more than three thousand years later, with no knowledge of the affairs of the office where they were written, the difficulties are immense, and it is no wonder if we have still many unsolved problems.

The following is a brief outline of how the syllabary is used to write words in this early dialect of Greek; but it is not possible here to go into much detail. All the vowels may be treated as either short or long; there is no separate notation, as in the later Greek alphabet, for long *e* and *o*. Initial *h*- is not usually written, but there is no reason to think that it was not pronounced. A vowel may be ignored when two, or even three, signs are written to represent a syllable containing a cluster of consonants, as *ti-ri-* for *tri-*. The letters *j* and *w* stand for the semivowels, the sounds we write in English as consonantal *y* and *w*. The *y* sound is generally absent from the later Greek language, though it may have been heard as a glide between the vowel *i* and an immediately following vowel. The signs *ja, je, jo, ju* are used in this way when another vowel follows an *i*. But they have a second use, to indicate that the preceding vowel is to be read as forming part of a diphthong in -*i*; so the ending -*o-jo* is to be read as answering to the Homeric -*oio*. The letter *w* stands for another sound which disappeared from later Greek, though early inscriptions of some dialects write it with a letter F, which survived by a remarkable series of changes to become the Roman letter we still know as *f*. The *w* sound was frequently to be found in the Mycenaean dialect of Greek. The letter *r* is a convention standing for either *r* or *l*.

The transcription *ka, ke, ki, ko, ku* is really a shorthand for any velar stop followed by these vowels. Greek has three velar stops, *k, kh* and *g* (written K, X and Γ in the later Greek alphabet), and the reader had to choose for himself which value to give the sign in any word. Likewise *pa, pe, pi,* etc. can stand for *p, ph* or *b*. But the series *ta, te, ti,* etc. stands only for *t*- or *th*-, and there is a separate series *da, de, di,* etc. for *d*-. The letter *q*- in transcription must be understood as *kw* (much like *qu*- in English *queen*), *khw* (the same with aspiration) and *gw* (as in *Gwen*). All of these sounds were lost before the classical period, when they were replaced according to

	a		*e*		*i*		*o*		*u*
	da		*de*		*di*		*do*		*du*
	ja		*je*				*jo*		*ju*
	ka		*ke*		*ki*		*ko*		*ku*
	ma		*me*		*mi*		*mo*		*mu*
	na		*ne*		*ni*		*no*		*nu*
	pa		*pe*		*pi*		*po*		*pu*
	qa		*qe*		*qi*		*qo*		
	ra		*re*		*ri*		*ro*		*ru*
	sa		*se*		*si*		*so*		*su*
	ta		*te*		*ti*		*to*		*tu*
	wa		*we*		*wi*		*wo*		
	za		*ze*				*zo*		

7 The basic Linear B syllabary

a₂		a₃		au	

8 The optional signs of Linear B

9 The unidentified signs of Linear B

context by *t* or *p*, *th* or *ph*, and *d* or *b*. Almost all classical words containing *b* come from an earlier *gw*, and it was facts like this which made the decipherment convincing to those acquainted with the history of the language. Difficult as it is for us, the system was no doubt clear enough to Mycenaean scribes; after all, we have no difficulty in giving six different values to the spelling *-ough* in different words (*though, through, thought, borough, tough, cough*).

Greek has only three consonants which can stand at the end of a word: *-n*, *-r* and *-s*. The use of final *-k* was restricted to certain special contexts, and probably did not occur in Mycenaean Greek. It was therefore possible to adopt the rule that final consonants should be omitted in writing. The same licence was extended to these sounds when they occurred in the middle of a word immediately followed by another consonant, and the same applied to the similar sounds *l* and *m* when they occurred in the same position. Double consonants are not indicated by the script, but they doubtless existed in speech. Other clusters of consonants have to be written by inserting extra vowels, which were not pronounced. The vowel *-i* as the second part of a diphthong (*ai, ei, oi, ui*) might be omitted, though it could optionally be inserted using the sign for *i*, or before another vowel by using the signs *ja, je, jo, ju*.

A few examples will show better how these rules work. These are isolated words, not a coherent text. The first line below gives the spelling as it occurs in the Linear B script. The second line gives the conventional transcription into syllables, separated by hyphens. The third line gives the phonetic form as we think it should be reconstructed from the syllables; letters in brackets have to be supplied by the reader. The fourth line gives an English translation of the word:

ka-ko	pa-ka-na	ti-ri-po	i-je-re-ja	qa-si-re-u
kha(l)ko(s)	pha(s)gana	tripo(s)	(h)iereia	gwasileu(s)
'bronze'	'swords'	'tripod'	'priestess'	'chief'

po-me	tu-ka-te	ko-wo	re-wo-to-ro-ko-wo
po(i)mē(n)	thugatē(r)	ko(r)wo(s)	lewotrokhowo(i)
'shepherd'	'daughter'	'boy'	'bath-pourers'

The use of the optional signs (fig. 8) needs to be explained. Some are straightforward, for instance *dwe*, *nwa* and *pte* are used in place of spellings with two signs: *de-we*, *nu-wa* and *pe-te*.

The sign a_2 is used in place of a to denote aspiration, that is, it is equivalent to *ha*. But it is optional, and *ha* is also written with the simple a. For example, a_2-*te-ro* is written for *hatero(n)*, 'other' (classical Greek *heteron*). But unlike later Greek this Mycenaean dialect used -*h*- between vowels in the middle of a word, and we have spellings like *pa-we*-a_2 (as well as *pa-we-a*) for *pharweha* (classical *pharē*), 'cloaks'. The sign a_3 is used only at the beginning of words and has the value *ai*-, as in a_3-*ku-pi-ti-jo*, a man's name, *Aiguptio(s)*, 'the Egyptian'. *au* is also restricted to the initial position; *au-ro* is for *aulo(i)*, 'pipes' (in this context, some part of a chariot).

The sign pu_2 normally has the value *phu*; *pu-te-re* is *phutēre(s)*, 'planters'. The exact values of ra_2 and ro_2 are disputed, but they were probably in origin *rya* and *ryo*, though by the date of our documents they may have advanced to *rra, (lla)* and *rro, (llo)*. ra_3 has the value *rai (lai)*; *e*-ra_3-*wo* is *elaiwo(n)* (classical *elaion*), 'olive-oil'.

The signs with the conventional values *za, ze, zo* pose a problem. The transcription was adopted because in many cases the corresponding classical words have the spelling *Z*, but at that date this letter had the value *zd*. There is good reason to think that in Mycenaean times these words were pronounced with the group reversed *dz*; so *to-pe-za* is *to(r)pedza* (classical *trapezda*), 'table'. But in other words *z*- appears to stand for *ts*, a group that was eliminated from all classical forms of Greek.

This difficulty is a good example of the kind of problems which arise as the result of our ignorance of this dialect of archaic Greek. If we had alphabetic spellings of the same date, it would be much easier to reconstruct the Mycenaean form. We can only do this by comparing the Mycenaean spelling with the alphabetic form of the same word, which may be as much as a thousand years later, and will in many cases have altered a great deal in the interval. In some cases we also need to take into account what we know of the earlier history of the word from a comparison of cognate words in other early languages. To take a very complicated case, the syllabic spelling *i-qo* can be reconstructed as *(h)i(k)kwo(i)*, 'horses', partly on the evidence of classical *hippoi*, but also of Latin *equi* and Sanskrit *aśvāḥ*. Although Linear B has answered some of our questions about Greek words, it has also left us with a lot of new ones.

It is quite certain that the Linear B script was borrowed from the earlier Linear A of Minoan Crete; this will be discussed in Chapter 5. Many of the signs are identical or very nearly so; but some are rather different in form, and there are some which appear in one script but not the other. Where and when the borrowing took place is unknown, but we have reason to think it may have been much earlier than the date of the Linear B tablets we have preserved. But this does not mean that even when the signs are the same, the values were necessarily also similar, though this is probably true in many cases. One reason for this is that in the course of time the pronunciation of words changes, and although sometimes a new spelling is introduced, there is a tendency to keep the old spelling but to give it the new value. Some of the appalling confusion of modern English spelling is due to this. In rather the same way, the Greeks may have modified the values of the signs that they took over from the Minoans; and we cannot be sure that they did not take the signs for which they had no use and give them totally unrelated values. Only a full decipherment of Linear A will resolve this question.

The difficulties in interpreting Linear B are not confined to those associated with the reconstruction of the phonetic forms. The 'Greek' of the Mycenaean period is quite certainly Greek, but it is far older than any other Greek known to us. The earliest alphabetic inscriptions belong to the eighth century BC, and our earliest literary source, the epic poems of Homer, were probably composed at the end of that same century. For some Mycenaean words we can only compare much later spellings. It is inevitable that between the end of the Mycenaean period, at the beginning of the twelfth century, and the time of Homer the language will have undergone drastic changes, not merely in pronunciation, but in the grammar and vocabulary.

We can classify the changes which languages undergo during the course of time into three types. We may find words which have changed their pronunciation. So in Greek the word for 'son' which was in Mycenaean *korwos* had become by the time of Homer *kouros; gwasileus*, 'chief', had become *basileus; newos*, 'new', had become *neos; lewotrokhowoi*, 'bath-pourers', had become *loutrokhooi; dleukos*, 'new wine', had become *gleukos*, and so on.

When we turn to grammar, we find changes have taken place in the inflexions. Mycenaean regularly has genitive endings in *-oio*, a poetic variant preserved by Homer, but replaced by *-ou* in standard Greek. It has a dative case in *-ei*, where later Greek uses *-i; di-we* is the dative of *Zeus, Diwei* for classical *Dïï*. The verb has a third person singular ending in the middle (or passive) voice *-toi* instead of *-tai; eukhetoi* for *eukhetai*, 'vows'. Some of our unsolved problems may be due to difficulties of this kind.

We may also encounter lexical changes. Over such a long period words tend to change their meanings, and new words have then to be found to express the original concept. Classical Greek has two words for 'king', *basileus* and *anax*, but the second of these is only used in poetic language, so it was known to be archaic. Mycenaean has *wanax*, the same word as *anax*, as its ordinary word for 'king'; but the equivalent of *basileus* is used in a wider sense, more like the English 'chief'. The Mycenaean word for 'wheel' is *harmo*, but the same word in the form *harma* means 'chariot' in later Greek, a development rather like our use of *wheels* to mean a vehicle. The Mycenaean word for 'chariot' is *hikkwiā*, literally 'the horse-(vehicle)', a word which disappeared from later Greek. Undoubtedly many other words died out in the gap between Mycenaean and our later texts; one reason for this may be the progress of technology, for new processes often demand new words. Similarly changes in political institutions call for the introduction of a new vocabulary.

Thus the interpretation of a Mycenaean word is hardly possible without a detailed knowledge of the history of the Greek language; it is little use looking up a classical lexicon to find the meaning of Mycenaean forms. There are, not surprisingly, still a number of words whose meaning we do not know for sure, though in some cases we can deduce from the context the approximate meaning.

When we turn to the ideograms, we have problems of quite a different kind. Some of these, as shown earlier, are recognisable at first sight. Others have become clear by identifying the contexts in which they were used. For example, one which appears with the Greek word for 'cloth' (fig. 10) was probably in origin a picture of an upright loom with weights at the bottom to keep the warp under tension. This identification is further confirmed by its association with the sign for 'wool', and this in turn is associated with the sign for 'sheep' (fig. 11).

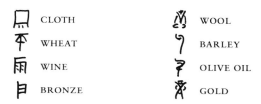

10   Some Linear B ideograms for commodities

Things like grain and liquids cannot of course be drawn recognisably, so the signs were probably intended as pictures of the plants which produced them. The signs for 'wheat' and 'barley' had in Linear B become merely conventional, but we can trace their origin back to Linear A, and there we find forms which look much more like the plants. Similarly 'wine' pictures a vine growing on a trellis, and 'olive oil' was probably to begin with a picture of an olive tree.

The domestic animals too are merely conventional forms, as they appear in Linear B (fig. 11).

11   Ideograms for domestic animals

The male sex is indicated by two cross-bars on the upright, the female sex by a divided upright; but the male forms are often used for the species as a whole, and may in some cases stand for castrated males. Any of these signs may be accompanied by syllabic signs used as abbreviations to denote special types, such as young, old, last year's and so on.

In some cases syllabic signs are used alone as ideograms. Some of these are straightforward abbreviations of Greek words; for instance, the word *o-pe-ro* meaning 'deficit', is often abbreviated to *o*. But others (fig. 12) are more interesting, since the syllabic value does not occur in the Greek name. These were probably taken over from Linear A, where the sound may have been that of the initial syllable of the name in the pre-Greek language of Crete. In fact, this is probably how the syllabary was invented, by using the pictogram of an object for the initial syllable of its name in that language.

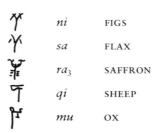

	ni	FIGS
	sa	FLAX
	ra₃	SAFFRON
	qi	SHEEP
	mu	OX

12 Syllabic signs also used as ideograms

The case of 'wool' (fig. 13), however, is more complicated. The skin of an animal may be roughly drawn, and then a syllabic sign inserted to suggest the Greek word; thus an ox-hide bears the sign for *wi* standing for *wrinos*, 'ox-hide'. But 'wool' belongs to the category of things which cannot be drawn recognisably. The solution chosen here goes back to Linear A; there two syllabic signs, *ma* and *ru*, were combined to form a ligature, presumably because this represented the name of 'wool' in that language.

LINEAR A   LINEAR B

13 The signs for 'wool' in Linear A and Linear B

Now it is probably no accident that Greek has a word *mallos* meaning 'flock of wool', which might well be borrowed from this pre-Greek language. But the ideogram of Linear B is no longer recognisable as a ligature, though it is very close to the syllabic sign *ma*.

But the principle of inventing an ideogram by stringing two or three syllabic signs together remained valid. We have several examples of this in Linear B, where the words are Greek and sometimes appear in syllabic spelling in the context (fig. 14).

	me-ri	$= meli$	'honey'
a-re-pa		$= aleiphar$	'ointment'
	tu-ro$_2$	$= turoi$	'cheeses'

14   Syllabic signs of ligatures

The metric signs are a special type of ideogram. There are three series; for weight, dry measure and liquid measure. The Mycenaeans must have also had a system of linear measure, but no trace of this appears in our documents.

Heavy materials such as bronze or lead are measured by the largest units of the system of weights; the smallest are used for such things as saffron. The signs and their relationships are shown in fig. 14.

15   The Linear B system of weights

The highest unit is clearly a picture of a pair of scales, and probably stands for the talent, the major unit of weight throughout antiquity. Its value varied widely, and until a satisfactory series of weights is found on a Mycenaean site we cannot hope to obtain a precise value. But there is reason to think that it was very roughly around 30 kg. The talent was divided into sixty *minas*, so the second largest unit, which has a double sign, was almost certainly a double-*mina*. The other units do not seem to correspond to those in later use. If the value for the talent suggested is about right, the smallest unit will come out at around 3.5 g.

The two systems of measurement of volume agree in their two lowest units. The next up is the same size in both systems, but has a different sign, which implies a different name. There is no sign for the highest unit in either system, but it is simply represented by the ideogram for the commodity directly followed by the numeral. Fig. 16 shows the two systems:

DRY MEASURE		LIQUID MEASURE	
⌣	× 4	⌣	× 4
= Þ	× 6	= Þ	× 6
= Τ	× 10	= ฯ	× 3
= 𐄷	(WHEAT)	= 𐄸	(WINE)

16   The volumetric systems of Linear B

The two lowest units stand in the same relationship as the classical *kotylē* and *khoinix*, but the higher ones are different. The determination of their values is much harder than in the case of the weights. No measuring vessels have been reliably identified from any Mycenaean site. The size of the smallest unit probably lies between 0·2 and 0·4 l., and there is some reason to prefer a value near the top of this range. This will give a major unit of up to 96 l. in dry measure, or 29 l. in liquid. The difference is probably due to the fact that a litre of wine weighs more than a litre of grain. The highest units may well represent the maximum load an average man could carry.

4
The Tablets as Historical Documents

The excavation of palaces in the Near East has revealed immense archives of tablets, far larger and more detailed than anything we have from Mycenaean Greece. But there have also been found among them annals, if not real histories, diplomatic correspondence, treaties, and even literary and religious texts. Linear B has produced nothing of the kind, and it may be doubted if the writing system was adequate to serve such purposes; it appears to have been devised solely as a means of keeping records, a way of extending the collective memory of the administrators.

Another major difference is that, unlike the Near Eastern tablets, Mycenaean tablets were never deliberately baked; they were accidentally baked in the fires that destroyed the buildings where they were kept, and in the absence of a fire no records survive. This means that at any one site we have only such tablets as were stored there at the time of the destruction. Moreover, there is a remarkable absence of dates on the tablets; only a small proportion have the name of a month, and years are only mentioned in such formulas as 'last year' or 'this year'. This implies that the tablets were rarely kept for more than a year; indeed, it seems likely that every winter the records of the past year were scrapped and a new collection begun. It is of course possible that on this occasion an abstract was transferred to some more expensive, but perishable, writing material; but if so, we have no trace of it.

It would seem at first sight almost impossible to glean any historical information from such records, and we must admit we know nothing about such matters as the names of kings or the lengths of their reigns. But within the limits imposed by the nature of the documents, it is possible to make some firm deductions and at least to advance hypotheses to explain the records. It is obvious that each tablet recorded a fact which was meaningful to the writer. Without his knowledge of the circumstances in which the tablet was written, we may find the record meaningless; but if we can conjecture the circumstances, we may be able to offer some explanation, or choose between different possible interpretations.

An example may help to explain this. Among the Pylos tablets is a large document (fig. 17) recording contributions of bronze from thirty-two officials all

17 Pylos tablet Jn 829,
listing contributions of bronze

over the kingdom. This bronze is described by a word which might mean 'of ships' or 'of temples'. The fact that some of the districts named are known to lie inland means that the official would be unlikely to have available 'ship bronze', whatever that might be. But temples, or rather small shrines, must have existed in all the major centres of population, and in later times we know that these were regularly furnished with vessels and other implements of bronze. Thus 'temple bronze' is the more likely interpretation, and this strongly suggests that the king was so short of metal he was demanding the surrender of temple property to help the war effort.

A further clue to the interpretation of the tablets is the possibility of grouping them into series. Very many tablets are exceedingly brief and laconic; in this they resemble single cards extracted from a card index, and they become meaningful only if we can reconstruct the file to which they belong. Some of these series were easily recognisable, especially by the ideograms they use, so that we could group together those listing, for instance, men, women, grain, oil, wine and other goods. But we can go further with this analysis, and here the study of handwriting has proved a valuable clue. As a rule, all the tablets belonging to the same file were written by the same scribe, while another superficially similar file was compiled by a different scribe. We can thus sometimes reconstruct the whole files, or rather baskets, into which the tablets were originally sorted; and the study of a whole file is infinitely more revealing than that of a single brief tablet. Of course tablets may well be missing from the file, and many that we have are damaged, so that our information is inevitably incomplete.

The tablets from Mycenae, Tiryns and Thebes are still too few to yield much useful information, but at least we can verify that they disclose the same sort of organisation as the two major archives, those of Pylos and Knossos. Generally speaking, the Pylos tablets are better organised and thus easier to interpret than those of Knossos; this might be due to their date, if the Knossos ones are really a century or more earlier. But despite differences it is clear that the system of administration was broadly similar in both kingdoms, and such evidence as we have from the other sites fits the picture we can build here.

We need of course to look at the tablets in the light of what we know of the geography of the region, and in some cases we can compare the records with the direct evidence of archaeology. But this has limits: for instance, most agricultural products leave little trace which can be detected archaeologically, and here the tablets can supply crucial information. There is, for example, nothing in the archaeological record of the south-west Peloponnese to suggest that flax was here an important crop. But the Pylos tablets reveal a highly organised textile industry based on flax; and this is strikingly confirmed by the fact that in modern times also much flax has been produced in this area.

The Pylos tablets confirm that Pylos (*pu-ro*) was the Mycenaean name of the site; but among the other place names there are few which can be located on the map. This is because in the period immediately following the destruction of the Palace around 1200 BC, the whole south-western Peloponnese seems to have suffered an abrupt decline in population. Thus many of the sites mentioned on the tablets were probably uninhabited for a time, and if they were later re-occupied, they then acquired new names. But there are a number of clues which enable us to guess the approximate location of the more important names. For instance, a number of names are listed as the location of coastguard units or as supplying rowers for the fleet; such place names must obviously be situated on or near the coast. There is also a standard order in which the major districts are listed; if we can relate that to the geography, we can deduce approximately where some of the areas must be.

We can now determine fairly accurately the limits of the kingdom administered by Pylos. It was divided into a Hither Province; the broad strip of habitable land down the west coast, and a Further Province, across the mountains in the fertile plain of Messenia. Each province was divided into districts, each of which had a governor and his deputy in charge. These sixteen districts are all listed on the tablet illustrated in fig. 17, together with the contributions of bronze required from the governor and deputy governor of each.

At Knossos the situation is a little better. Apart from Knossos itself (*ko-no-so*), we can recognise the names of Amnisos, its harbour, Phaistos, the major site in the south of the island, Lyktos a little further to the east, and Kydonia (the modern Khania) in the far west. There are a number of other names which may be the early form of known Cretan towns. There is a mention of Mount Dikte, already associated with the worship of Zeus. But the picture that has emerged seems to exclude the eastern end of the island, and the kingdom of Knossos seems to have been based on the main central section with some sort of control extending to the western end only.

At neither site is the king mentioned by name; we have only the title 'the king' (*wa-na-ka*). He had an important officer who may have been his second-in-command, perhaps the chief of the army. His court was composed of officers called 'Followers' (*e-qe-ta*), or as we might say 'Companions'.

Some tablets appear to record large quantities of wheat; but it is clear that most of these documents are really lists of persons holding land, which is measured in seed-corn. The holders of land clearly had obligations to fulfil in return for their holding, for we have notes that some of them had not met their obligations; these probably included military service in time of war.

There was no currency in use, but the Palace appears to have paid its workers in kind. Two files of tablets at Pylos list women workers who receive rations of wheat and figs (fig. 18). Some of the women are domestics, such as the 'bath-pourers' already mentioned, who were probably responsible for the functions discharged in modern times by plumbing. But the majority seem to have been workers in the textile industry, producing woollen and linen cloth of various kinds. Other tradesmen are listed as receiving quantities of food and drink.

18   Pylos tablet Ab 573, listing sixteen women of Miletus, with three girls and seven boys, and a ration of wheat and figs

At Knossos something like a third of all the tablets in the archive are concerned with sheep and wool. Each card in the file records the name of the person responsible for the flock, its location, size and in some cases make-up. Other files record the difference between the actual numbers and the nominal strength, most being a round hundred. Yet other tablets record the wool clip, showing deficiencies below the target figure. In Crete at least the production of wool was highly organised; and there too the Palace controlled groups of female workers, who spun the yarn, wove and decorated the cloth. The linen industry was a speciality of the Pylos area.

These women are not specifically called 'slaves', but their status can hardly have been much higher. Other workers are specifically called by this title, but perhaps the distinction between slave and free was not so rigidly drawn as in later Greece. There are also slaves (or servants) of various deities, but some of these seem to have been of higher status.

Wheat and barley both figure prominently on the tablets. Other agricultural produce listed includes figs, olives, olive oil and wine, all still staple items in the diet of the Greek peasant. Apart from sheep, we have records of goats, pigs and oxen; but oxen are not numerous, and seem to have been largely used for traction. This is surely true of the tablets at Knossos which list yokes of oxen, giving not only the name of their driver but actually those of the oxen too.

19   Knossos tablet Ch 897, showing the name of an ox-driver and his two charges

Many series of tablets are concerned with manufactured goods, either listed as in the Palace storerooms or as being produced for the Palace. There was a system by which raw materials were issued to workers, and a careful record was kept of the quantities each received. This is clearly seen at Pylos, where bronze was allotted to groups of smiths, whose names were listed, though what they were required to make with it is not given. The contributions of 'temple bronze' mentioned above are specifically said to be for points for javelins and spears. Weapons as well as tools must have been an important part of the production.

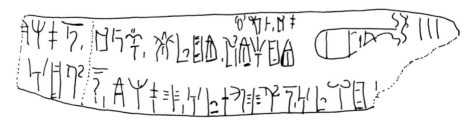

20   Knossos tablet Sd 4403, with a description of three chariot-bodies

At Knossos we have detailed descriptions of chariots, a regular piece of military equipment at that time. Some of them are elaborately decorated, painted red and inlaid with ivory. The wheels are listed separately; they are described as made of elm or willow, but some have bronze or even silver fittings.

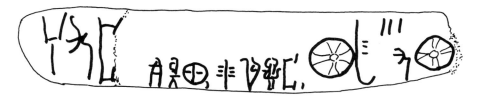

21   Knossos tablet So 4439, listing three pairs and one single wheel made of willow

There are also records of body armour, though the material it is made of is not specified. A complete set of bronze armour has been found in a tomb of Mycenaean date, but it would seem that the type listed at Pylos was made of some material such as linen or leather with bronze plates sewn on to reinforce it. Fig. 19 shows a Pylos tablet recording five pairs of old corslets, each with twenty large and ten small plates, and with four plates for the helmet and two for cheek-pieces. 'Old' probably means no more than 'not newly made'.

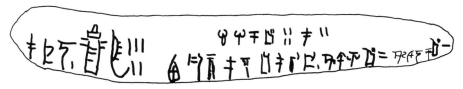

22   Pylos tablet Sh 740, showing armour

There are lists of leather goods mentioning equipment such as harness and trappings for horses, and listing the skins of deer as well as of domestic animals. Some of these were used for making footwear.

In many ways the most interesting document is a set of tablets from Pylos which begins with a heading stating that these objects were inspected when a certain important official was appointed by the king. The list begins with vessels, probably of bronze, which are described by their decoration; among them are six tripod-cauldrons. One of these tablets, where the drawing of a three-legged vessel is clear, was mentioned above as having proved the validity of the decipherment. There are also fire-rakes and tongs, axes and swords. But the list then goes on to describe a collection of furniture. There are 'thrones', i.e. formal chairs of state, decorated with ivory, lapis lazuli and gold, and a larger number of stools, possibly foot-stools, but perhaps also used as seats, equally decorated. Then there is a collection of ten tables, all described in detail and elaborately decorated. The translation of these descriptions is difficult, but there is no doubt that this is a sumptuous collection of precious items. The whole list must be an inventory of a palace storeroom for valuables.

It is surprising that although there was plenty of evidence found in the excavation of the Palace at Pylos to show that no expense had been spared on its construction and decoration, hardly any portable objects of value were found in it. This strongly suggests that before the disastrous fire which destroyed it, the Palace had been deliberately stripped of valuable goods. This would happen if it had been captured by a raiding party, looted and then set on fire. We are therefore justified in asking whether the Pylos tablets give any indication of a state of emergency.

There is no direct evidence, but a number of documents offer indirect evidence, which, taken together, certainly constitute a proof that Pylos was expecting an attack coming from the sea. The most telling is a series of tablets which records the establishment of a coastguard organisation. Some have argued that in default of information about regular practice, this cannot be regarded as proof of an emergency. It would nevertheless be very remarkable if a kingdom of this size could in normal times produce a force of some eight hundred men to keep watch on the coastline. It is clearly not a defensive force, since there are about a hundred miles of coastline, so the force works out at, on average, one man for each 220 yds; and it would be absurd to split the force up into small units, some of only ten men.

Fig. 23 shows the first of five similar tablets dealing with this subject. The first line is a heading which translates: 'As follows the watchers are guarding the coastal

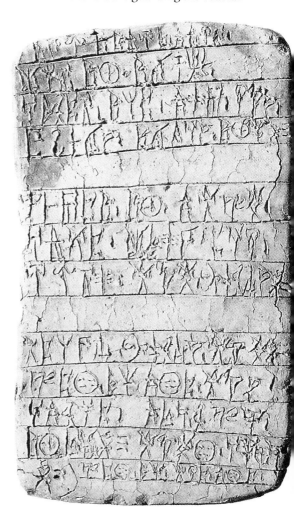

23   Pylos tablet An 657, showing
the coastguard organisation

area.' Then the commands of two officers are described, giving the force at their disposal and their location together with the names of their subordinate officers. Eight other commands are listed on the other four tablets of the series. In the case of the second command on this tablet (line 6) it is known that the two men named as the commander and his first subordinate are almost certainly the governor and vice-governor of one of the districts in the north of the kingdom. The men under their command are described partly as natives of a particular town, but also by proper names which sound like non-Greek tribal or ethnic names. The men used for this purpose may therefore not have been full citizens.

At the end of the tablet we have an entry stating that a certain 'Follower', an officer of the royal court, was with them. These Followers are rather curiously distributed among the districts, and they seem to be concentrated in the area nearest to the Palace. It is therefore a fair guess that they were in fact in command of the military forces in each area, and the army has been stationed where it is best placed to repel attacks on the main centres of population.

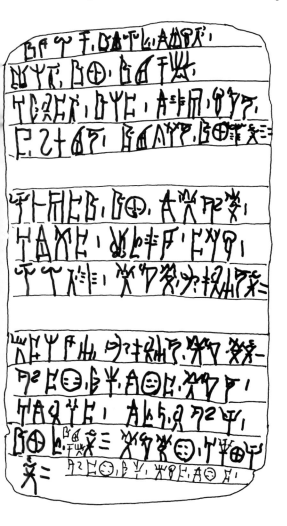

A defensive system based on the coast must obviously envisage an attack from the sea, but there is no indication who the expected enemy might be. There are in fact only two reasonable routes by which a land force could attack: either coming down the west coast, where there is a pass which could fairly easily be held, or by a much more difficult route through the mountains of Arcadia. We should therefore expect the Pylians to have manned their fleet, so when we find a document recording about six hundred men who are to serve as rowers, it is reasonable to infer that this is the expected mobilisation of the ships. There is even another tablet which records that small numbers of those due to serve in the fleet have been excused.

Another piece of evidence has already been mentioned, the document (fig. 17) recording the collection of temple bronze from every district in the kingdom. This is specifically said to be 'for points for javelins and spears', that is to say, scrap metal was being requisitioned for the making of armaments. Another document, which is hardly likely to be a normal demand, records the payment of large quantities of gold by local governors and other important officials; the tablet is damaged and some of the figures are lost, but the total comes to the astonishing sum of more than five kg. Wealth on this scale can hardly have been requisitioned annually; it only makes sense if this is a 'one-off' levy for the war.

But the most striking document is that shown in fig. 24. Religious offerings are quite a common type of entry, since the Palace was obviously responsible for maintaining the local shrines. We have lists from Knossos of the issue of olive oil, honey and other goods to various addresses, one of which is the celebrated cave of Eileithyia at Amnisos, well known both from Homer and its archaeological finds. There are similar mentions at Pylos of perfumed oils being sent to addresses, some of which are clearly religious institutions. But the tablet discussed here is unique.

It was, as the illustration shows, written on both sides. This is unusual, though on occasion a scribe, having miscalculated the length of his text, does allow it to run over onto the back or even the edge. Generally, however, a second tablet is written to contain the surplus. What is worse, the scribe here began his draft with blank lines which were never filled. Moreover, there are signs of erasure all over the tablet, and it looks as if it was originally written, then deleted and re-used for the present text. What is now the beginning is written on what was originally the back of the tablet. Even when he wrote the final text, the scribe made obvious mistakes, since in writing formulas that occur several times he omitted signs which are clearly needed. What he wrote is in places exceedingly difficult to read, and this is not entirely due to subsequent damage to the tablet. Altogether the impression given is that of a hasty draft, and had the tablet been stored in the archive room for any length of time, we should have expected a clean copy to have been made, so that this could be destroyed. Since it was not, we may well assume it to have been written in the last days, if not hours, before the Palace was destroyed.

It begins with a date and a place; it is a place name we only know from the tablets, but it is probably the name of the district within which the Palace lay, since the name 'PYLOS' is written six times in large signs at the left. The formula used is not

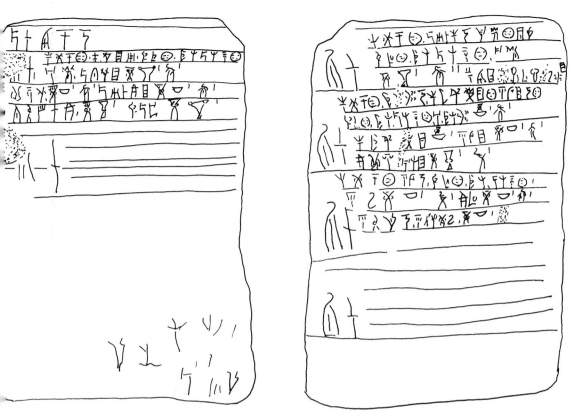

24 Pylos tablet Tn 316, written on both sides, obviously badly drafted and incomplete

wholly clear, but it refers to the bringing of gifts and an unknown word, which seems to mean something like 'victims'. Then after each repetition of the introductory formula we have a list of deities, some familiar such as Zeus, Hera and Hermes, but also including many more obscure names and titles. Each entry ends with a pictogram showing a cup or other vessel, preceded by the ideographic sign for 'gold' and followed by the numeral 1. Each deity is receiving a gold vessel, and since there are no less than thirteen of them, this can hardly be a regular ritual. The scribe began by drawing each cup differently, but as he went on he tired of this and used a simple conventional outline. But in nine of the entries the gold cup is followed by the mention of a human being; most often one woman, but once two women, and twice one man. The women are associated with female deities, the men with male ones. Whether these unlucky people were to be human sacrifices or merely given over to divine service we cannot be sure; but since early Greek legends often refer to human sacrifice, we cannot suppose it was unknown at this period. There is also some archaeological evidence from other sites which points the same way. But if it was a sacrifice of ten human beings at once, it surely suggests an extreme emergency. This ceremony was probably being planned in a last-minute attempt to invoke divine aid, and perhaps the blow fell before it could be carried out.

5
Linear A

Sir Arthur Evans distinguished three types of script used in Crete during the Bronze Age. The latest of these, Linear B, has been deciphered as already shown, but some account must be given of the earlier scripts, although these are not yet fully deciphered. Evans named these 'pictographic' or 'hieroglyphic' from a superficial resemblance to the hieroglyphic script of Egypt, and Linear A, because in this the pictograms of the earlier form had been reduced to simple outlines.

Generally speaking hieroglyphic inscriptions are earlier than the Linear A examples; but there is a much more striking difference in the material on which they usually appear. By far the largest number of hieroglyphic inscriptions are on seal-stones or sealings; only rarely are they found incised with a stylus on clay. Linear A is used either on clay tablets or on objects made of hard materials such as stone or metal. We are probably right in regarding Linear A as a later development of hieroglyphic, but the line between them is sometimes hard to discern.

25   The four faces of a seal from near Lyttos

The number of Linear A inscriptions known is still relatively small, a fraction of the number in Linear B. Moreover, a comparison based upon the number of signs rather than documents increases the disproportion, since so many Linear A documents are short or ill-preserved. It is therefore not surprising that much less progress has been made towards the decipherment of Linear A.

The largest collection of Linear A clay tablets comes from the Minoan palace of Haghia Triada, very close to Phaistos, in the south of Crete. But tablets or fragments of tablets have been found all over the island, and we can assume that this script was in general use for accounting purposes in Crete. So far as the evidence goes, it appears to represent the same language wherever found. Scraps of tablets have also been found in two of the Aegean islands to the north, Melos and Kea.

The same script has been found incised on portable objects of stone, pottery or metal. Here too the distribution is widespread in Crete, and there is a vessel from Thera in the south Aegean. A few inscriptions have been claimed for mainland Greece, or more remote areas; these are all too short for real certainty, and we can safely conclude that Linear A was the script of the Minoan civilisation of Crete and its overseas possessions, thus probably including at least the southern Aegean.

The chronological limits are not easy to define, but 'hieroglyphic' inscriptions are not earlier than the Middle Minoan period (roughly 1900–1600 BC). Towards the end of this period the more simplified forms appear, and Linear A was probably evolved around the eighteenth century. It continued in use until the collapse of the Minoan civilisation in the middle of the fifteenth century. Attempts made to date any Linear A document after this have so far proved vain.

The direction of the script is, so far as can be determined, from left to right. But a few signs are occasionally written reversed as in a mirror, and this suggests that it may perhaps at one time have been used also in the right-to-left direction.

It is immediately obvious that the Linear A script is very closely related to Linear B. The signary is of roughly the same size, and it is used in a similar way. Many of the signs are identifiable with corresponding Linear B ones, though there are some which are unknown to Linear B, and some Linear B signs have no clear ancestors in Linear A. The ideograms too are very similar, so that we can usually form a good idea of the contents of a Linear A tablet. The numerical system is the same, though less formally arranged; the tens may be written as heavy dots as well as bars. There is a major difference in the system of measurement, for although some of the metric signs of Linear B recur, they do not fall into the same patterns. Indeed it is clear the Linear A had a system of fractions, where Linear B uses the next lower unit in the system; but owing to the lack of sufficient well preserved texts, it is still impossible to give values to most of the signs in this class.

There is a certain crudity in presentation to be seen on Linear A tablets which contrasts with the tidier habits of Linear B scribes. Most Linear A tablets are of page shape, but are much smaller than most Linear B tablets of this type. The lines of writing are not usually divided by horizontal lines; and what is worse, separate entries are not tabulated by starting each on a new line. The scribes felt no difficulty in breaking a word at the end of a line, or putting the relevant numeral at the beginning of the next line. It is therefore much more difficult to analyse the pattern of entries, or even to see where one ends and the next begins. But it is clear that the nature and purpose of most tablets was similar to those of the Linear B variety; they are accounts of men and women, animals and produce, of much the same type, even if less detailed.

It is tempting to suppose that we can give the signs the values of the corresponding ones in Linear B. It would after all be perverse to borrow a script, but then to give the signs totally new values. So we should expect most of the signs common to both scripts to have the same, or similar, values. But the analogy of modern alphabets warns us of the danger in taking this approach too far. Some of the letters of the Cyrillic alphabet used for Russian look like English ones; but we know that B, C, P, X and Y, for example, have different values in the Cyrillic script. Since we know the values in both scripts, and we can trace their history over a long period, these differences can be explained. But if we knew nothing of the values in Cyrillic, it would be very difficult to correct the false ideas we should have gained from English.

It was therefore necessary to test the assumption of similar values and see if they could be proved or disproved. There is not enough evidence to complete the proof; but so far as it goes the results are encouraging. The same word seems in certain cases to be spelled either with initial *a*- or initial *ja*-; not only are the sounds very much alike, but we have a similar alternation in Linear B. Many of the entries on the tablets are clearly personal names; if they are decoded on the Linear B model, we find a number which are almost identical with names found on the Knossos Linear B tablets. It might be expected that some of the names in use in Minoan Crete would have survived the Greek conquest. Significantly, those ending in -*u* in Linear A often appear in Linear B ending in -*o*, a change which may well be due to fitting a foreign name into a Greek declensional type. In fact the vowel *o* has a much lower, and *u* a much higher frequency than in Linear B.

Since the structure of most tablets is very similar to that familiar in Linear B, we can apply the same methods to the decipherment. A tablet from the south Cretan site of Haghia Triada will show the possibilities (fig. 26).

The analysis of this tablet is not difficult. The first line is a heading, very likely a place name. The second line begins with a sign identical to the Linear B ideogram for 'wine'. Then follows an isolated sign, which appears to mean something like 'paid out', or 'issued'. After this comes a list of six words, probably personal names, each followed by a numeral, presumably therefore specifying the amout of wine each received. There is a sign after some numerals which must indicate the fraction $\frac{1}{2}$. Some of the figures are slightly damaged, but they can probably be restored as: $5\frac{1}{2}$, 56, $27\frac{1}{2}$, $17\frac{1}{2}$, 19, 5. The last line has a word (made up of two signs) which regularly appears on tablets in this position, followed by the numeral $130\frac{1}{2}$. Since this is the total of the preceding figures, the word before it must effectively mean 'total', 'so much' or the like.

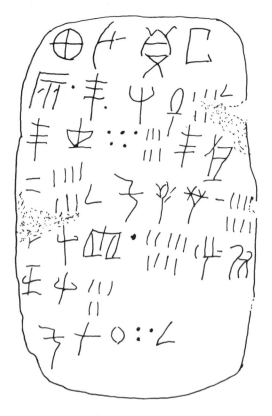

26   Haghia Triada tablet 13   27   Haghia Triada tablet 85, side *a*

In fig. 27 we have a very similar list, but the commodity counted is, apparently, men, since the first line ends with the ideogram for 'man'. The seven separate entries may be place names or descriptive titles, or even persons to whom the groups of men are assigned. Again the total is given with the same formula as in the previous example. Unfortunately many of the tablets are fragmentary or damaged, and their interpretation is thus less certain.

But there is one deduction which is immediately possible: the language cannot be Greek. The word for 'total', if transcribed with the Linear B values, comes out as *ku-ro*, which is not only quite different from the Linear B *to-so*, but cannot be reconstructed as any Greek word of suitable meaning. There are only a few words like this, the meaning of which can be deduced from the context; and although attempts have been made to connect these with words in other languages, especially Semitic, no convincing set of parallels has yet been demonstrated. We need more texts, especially more detailed ones, if we are to make much more progress here.

But we do also have inscriptions of a type not so far found in Linear B, those on movable objects. Many of these are what the archaeologists call 'libation tables', large stone dishes apparently used for offerings to deities. There are also inscriptions on metal objects. These have a quite different structure from the tablets. There are usually no ideograms and no numerals to give a clue to the subject matter. The parallel of classical Greek inscriptions on similar objects suggests that these are religious dedications. They probably record the name of the deity to whom they are offered, that of the donor, and sometimes other details like the reason for making the offering. A number of inscriptions repeat the same words, but which are divine names and which dedicatory formulas is still not clear.

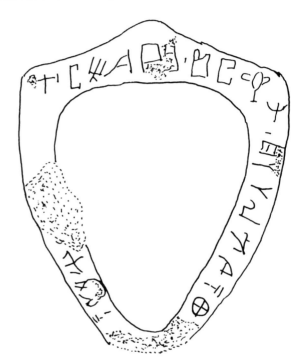

28   Stone ladle from Troullos

A stone ladle from Troullos (fig. 28) is a good example. The first word reappears in various forms at the beginning of inscriptions on other objects, such as libation tables. The right-hand edge begins with a word which, if we apply the Linear B values, reads *ja-sa-sa-ra-me*. The word *a-sa-sa-ra*, with *a-* replacing *ja-*, recurs on a number of such inscriptions, and has been suspected of being a divine name or title.

A silver pin from Platanos also has an inscription of the same votive type, but the newly discovered gold pin (fig. 29) does not repeat any of the regular formulas and therefore remains obsure.

29   A gold pin of unknown origin (now in Haghios Nikolaos Museum)

Lastly we may notice a few incised inscriptions on vessels, the most notable of which is an enormous jar, some five feet high, which has an inscription written in two lines running between the handles. It was found in the Minoan palace of Kato Zakros on the east coast of Crete. The interesting feature here is that the inscription begins with the sign for 'wine' followed by the numeral '32'. If this indicates the capacity and means that it was intended for storing wine, this would certainly provide for a heroic drinking-party, but the second line begins with a variant form of the dedicatory formula, so the meaning of the whole text still remains unclear.

6
The Cypriot Connection

It has long been known that the island of Cyprus, standing on the eastern edge of the Greek world, had a script of its own in use during the classical period. Its decipherment was made easy by the discovery of a number of short inscriptions giving the same text in the local script and in the Greek alphabet. This revealed that the local dialect of the Greek language was written by means of a simple syllabic script, of the same type as that used in Linear B. A connection between it and the 'Minoan' script was suggested by Evans as early as 1894, and he later proposed that the Bronze Age script of Cyprus should be known as Cypro–Minoan. However, only a few short inscriptions of this date were known until fragments of large clay tablets were found at the site of Enkomi, on the east coast of Cyprus, in 1952–3.

The earliest true inscription from Cyprus so far known was discovered at Enkomi in 1955. It is a piece of a large thick clay tablet, containing only three lines of writing. Although some of the signs are unlike anything in Linear A or B, it was immediately obvious that most showed a distinct resemblance. This discovery proved what had already been predicted, that the source of the Cypriot system was Cretan Linear A, not Greek Linear B, for the date of this fragment is around 1500

30   Clay tablet from Enkomi, c.1500 BC

BC, considerably earlier than anything known in Linear B, but contemporary with Linear A. No progress is possible with this early script so long as evidence for it remains so poor.

The other fragments of clay tablets found at Enkomi belong to a later period, the late thirteenth or twelfth centuries BC. They belong to the large, thick type of tablet used for literary as well as record purposes in the Near East. The script is much changed by this date, and the signs have become simple patterns of lines, probably evolved as the result of habitual use on clay, rather than directly influenced by cuneiform, which had undergone a similar evolution at a much earlier date. There can be no doubt that this script, now generally known as Cypro–Minoan, is descended from a Cretan original; but the equation of signs is often highly problematic, and it is quite impossible to make much progress by means of the clues afforded by Linear A.

In recent times the number of examples of Cypro–Minoan inscriptions has increased, though most of the new discoveries are very short. A frequent type is a small clay ball bearing a few signs. There is also an example of a clay cylinder bearing a longer inscription. What was the function of these objects remains obscure, and without some clue it is impossible to guess the content of such inscriptions.

31   Fragment of a large clay tablet from Enkomi, c.1200 BC

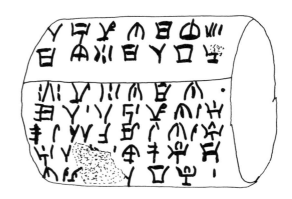

32 Clay cylinder from Enkomi

What has now emerged from the detailed study of this material, especially by Emilia Masson of Paris, is that the tablets use a different variety of the script from the other objects. The significance of this variation is not clear, but the suspicion must arise that the two scripts were used to write different languages. To add to the confusion, a third variety has now appeared on a clay tablet found, not in Cyprus, but at the site of the ancient city of Ugarit on the coast of Syria. This document has been plausibly interpreted as a list of names of Semitic character, which is not suprising since the local language of Ugarit is a Semitic dialect. It does not, however, afford proof that the language of Cypro–Minoan was itself Semitic, and this in fact appears improbable.

Further progress with Cypro–Minoan can be expected, if more examples are found. It would seem likely that more exploration of the important Bronze Age site at Enkomi would yield more tablets of the type already known, and it must be hoped that a solution of the problems that beset the island will soon enable archaeological work to be resumed in areas at present under Turkish occupation.

The Greek colonisation of the island was reported by tradition as beginning after the Trojan War, and there is archaeological evidence for a new people in Cyprus, especially in the west, from about the twelfth century BC. The temple of Aphrodite at Paphos in the south-west was throughout the classical period an important cult site, and Aphrodite was often referred to in Greece as simply 'the Cyprian goddess'. It is from this area that the earliest examples have come of the later Cypriot syllabic script. This remained in use by all the Greek cities of the island throughout the classical period. Although the Greek alphabet was devised, probably in the early eighth century BC, on models derived from Phoenicia, the coast of modern Syria and Lebanon, the Cypriots resisted this innovation, until the spread of the Macedonian empire under Alexander the Great led to the adoption of the standard script of the Greek world.

There can be no doubt about the Minoan origin of this classical script, since not only are some simple signs identical, or almost so, to the Minoan ones, but they have the same values as the corresponding sign in Linear B (fig. 33). In many more cases it is possible to trace some resemblance between signs having the same value and to suggest how they may have evolved. It must be remembered that the script must have been in use over a period of a thousand years, and it is not surprising that many signs show little resemblance.

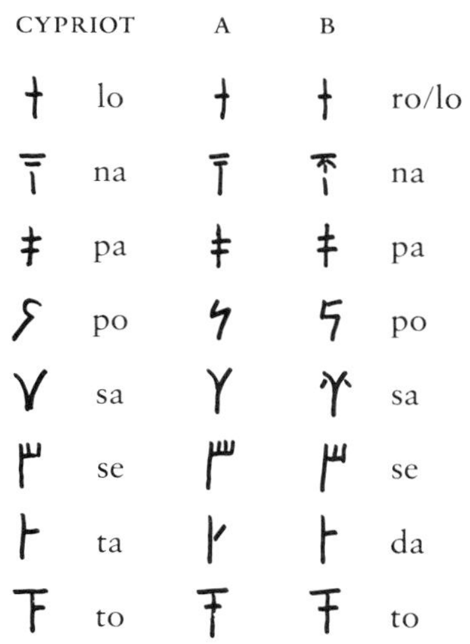

Cypriot		A	B	
†	lo	†	†	ro/lo
⊤̄	na	⊤̄	�‏	na
‡	pa	‡	‡	pa
ƒ	po	↳	↳	po
Υ	sa	Υ	Υ̇	sa
Ͱ	se	Ͱ	Ͱ	se
⊦	ta	⊬	⊦	da
Ŧ	to	Ŧ	Ŧ	to

33   A comparison of classical Cypriot signs with Linear A and Linear B

The syllabary is organised on much the same lines as that of Linear B. The reason for this is not only their common origin, but the fact that they were devised for the same language, even if different dialects of it. Again we have a system with five vowels, since this is what the language demands. The consonants are slightly different: the labio-velar (*q-*) series has disappeared due to changes in the pronunciation of these words; *t* and *d* are no longer distinguished, but *l* and *r* are.

But the main difference is not in the structure of the syllabary, but in its use. No longer is it judged sufficient to write a skeletal notation, which the reader has to fill in for himself; for true inscriptions the script needs to be more complete. The final consonants, -*n*, -*r*, -*s*, are noted by using *ne*, *re* and *se*. All groups of consonants are spelled out using extra vowels as necessary; and equally all diphthongs are spelled out. The only exception is that the nasals (*n* or *m*) are omitted before another consonant. Although a divider is used between groups of signs, this is not always employed at the end of each word, some phrases being treated as a single group. A few examples will illustrate how the system works:

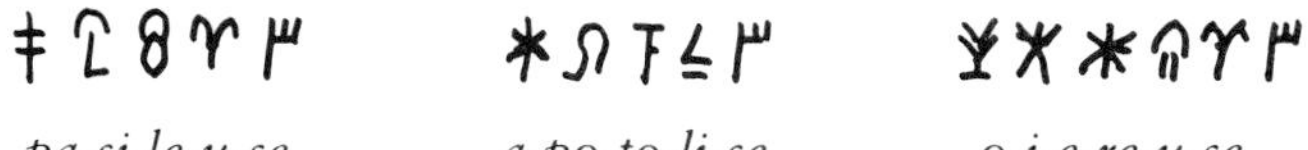

‡ ⌒ 8 Υ Ͱ   ✳ ∩ Ŧ ⅃ Ͱ   ⅄ ✕ ✳ ⌒ Υ Ͱ

pa-si-le-u-se   *a-po-to-li-se*   *o-i-e-re-u-se*

basileus   *hā ptolis*   *ho hiereus*

'king'   'the city'   'the priest'

Ⅴ ⊦ ⌂ ⨦ ƒ ⅀ Ͱ   Ŧ ⫽ ⅍ ∏ ⅚

sa-ta-si-ku-po-ro-se   *to-no-ro-ko-ne*

Stāsikupros   *ton horkon*

(man's name)   'the oath'

A further difference concerns the direction of writing. The most common direction is from right-to-left, though there are some examples of left-to-right. This is surprising in view of the left-to-right direction of Cypro–Minoan; it may be that the reverse direction is due to Semitic influence.

There are minor differences in the forms of the signs in use at different sites. The table (fig. 34) gives normalised forms only:

a e i o u
ja jo
ka ke ki ko ku
la le li lo lu
ma me mi mo mu
na ne ni no nu
pa pe pi po pu
ra re ri ro ru
sa se si so su
ta te ti to tu
wa we wi wo
xa xe zo
ga

34 The Cypriot syllabary; the values *xa*, *xe* and *zo* are not entirely certain; *ga* is only used at certain sites

The earliest inscription so far found in this script comes from Palaipaphos in the south-west, where a tomb of the eleventh century BC yielded three bronze spits, one of which bears an inscription. It reads from left to right: *o-pe-le-ta-u*. This makes good sense as *Opheltau*, the genitive of a familiar Greek name *Opheltes*. It is quite common for objects to be inscribed with the owner's name, and this is usually in the genitive case, as we might write *John's*. What is interesting about this inscription, besides the very early date, is that the form of the genitive is characteristic of the Cypriot dialect as known later on, but is slightly different from the Mycenaean. At least it seems to prove the very high antiquity of the Greek colonisation of Cyprus.

There is no other inscription so far known before the eighth century, and they only become at all common in the sixth century. Unfortunately most of these are from funerary monuments and contain nothing but the name of the deceased. There are also a number of dedicatory inscriptions which are not much more informative. In the fifth century, however, we have an important document from the city of Idalion. It is a large bronze tablet (fig. 35) engraved on both sides with a long inscription. It records a contract entered into by 'the king and the city' and gives a reward to a family of physicians who had operated a free health service for the casualties, when the city was besieged by the Persians. It reads from right to left and

35   The Idalion bronze tablet of the fifth century BC

is very well preserved; there are only a few problems caused by the unfamiliar dialect. The following is an extract:

a-no-ko-ne-o-na-si-lo-ne / *to-no-na-si-ku-po-ro-ne*

anōgon   Onasilon   ton   Onasikuprōn

they ordered Onasilos the (son) of Onasikupros

to-ni-ja-te-ra-ne / *ka-se* / *to-se* / *ka-si-ke-ne-to-se* /

ton iatēran   kas   tos   kasignētos

the physician   and   the   brothers

i-ja-sa-ta-i / *to-se* / *a-to-ro-po-se* / *to-se* / *i-ta-i*

iasthai   tos   a(n)thrōpos   tos   i(n) tāi

to heal   the   men   those   in   the

ma-ka-i / *i-ki-ma-me-no-se* / *a-ne-u* / *mi-si-to-ne*

makhāi   ikmamenos   aneu   misthōn

battle   wounded   without   fee

This script continued in use down to the Hellenistic period, but at that date obviously many people were unable to read and write it, so inscriptions are found with the text in both Cypriot script in dialect, and in the Greek alphabet in the standard form of the language. An example is given in fig. 36.

36 Cypriot inscription in two scripts, a dedication by Ellowoikos to Demeter and Kore

7

The Phaistos Disk

A book dealing with the pre-alphabetic scripts of the Aegean area cannot avoid mentioning the most famous document so far discovered in Crete. In 1908 an Italian excavator found in the ruins of the first palace at Phaistos in southern Crete a large disk of baked clay, covered on both sides by an inscription. Its date is given by its archaeological context as not later than about 1700 BC. It is therefore contemporary with Linear A, and it has been generally assumed to be a specimen of another script of the same family. While it is certainly an inscription, it is very questionable whether it belongs to the Minoan family, for it is in at least one respect unique.

The disk has the distinction of being the world's first typewritten document. It was made by taking a stamp or punch bearing the sign to be written in a raised pattern, and impressing this on the wet clay. The maker therefore needed to have as many stamps as there were signs in the script. It has the advantage that even complicated signs can be quickly written, and every example of the same sign is identical and easy to read. The disadvantage is that a considerable outlay of time and effort is required to make the set of stamps before any document can be produced. It is therefore evident that the system was not created solely for a single document; its maker must have intended to produce a large number of documents, though it remains some way from being an anticipation of printing.

It is therefore all the more remarkable that after more than eighty years of excavation not another single scrap of clay impressed with these stamps has been found at Phaistos, or at any other site in Crete or elsewhere. It would be very surprising if there were not somewhere more examples of the script waiting to be found, but the disk remains so far unique, and the suspicion must arise that it was an isolated object brought from some other area.

This impression of foreign origin can be supported by two arguments. The work of cutting the stamps, whether made directly or perhaps more likely by making moulds into which metal was poured, is a technique very similar to gem-engraving. We might therefore expect the signs to bear a stylistic resemblance to those engraved on seal-stones. In fact the style of art is noticeably different. Secondly,

37   The Phaistos Disk, side *b*

some of the objects pictured by the signs have a distinctly foreign appearance to those familiar with Minoan art.

38   Signs on the Phaistos Disk

Helmets with crests, as shown in the first sign on fig. 34, are not Minoan, though they were used at a rather later date by the Philistines. The woman sign shows a female dress quite different from that favoured by the Minoans. The third sign is hard to interpret, but it is an object unknown from any Minoan context, though it bears a striking resemblance to a form of sarcophagus, itself probably modelled on a house, in use later among the Lycians, a people of south-west Anatolia.

Comparison with Minoan hieroglyphic and Linear A inscriptions discloses some resemblances between signs; but since both scripts are obviously pictographic in origin, it is not surprising if two pictures of the same object look alike. None of the more complicated and thus distinctive signs can be paralleled. Its Minoan origin must thus rest in doubt until more evidence is available.

Although the origin of the disk is so uncertain, it has the great advantage of being easily legible, since it has suffered very little damage. Both faces of the disk are completely covered with writing arranged in a spiral pattern; the disk was presumably rotated as it was written, so that the bottom of the sign is nearest to the rim. The absence of blank spaces must be the result of practice and careful planning, unless of course this is one of a series of disks containing a long text, and what we have is, so to speak, a page out of a book.

The direction of the script has been hotly disputed, and many people have assumed that it reads from left to right like the other Minoan scripts. But it has now been firmly established that in some places one sign very slightly overlaps that to its right. It follows that the maker worked from right to left, and therefore from the rim towards the centre. It is just possible, but obviously highly improbable, that the reader was expected to read the text in the reverse direction. The signs which represent human beings and animals in profile are shown facing the right, which would be natural with a script running leftwards. It is also clear that the signs round the rim were written first, and there is some irregularity where the spiral leaves the rim and begins to run above the outermost line.

The disk is about 6¼ in (160 mm) in diameter and about ½ in (12 mm) thick. There is a total of 242 signs on the two faces. These are arranged into 61 groups, each demarcated by lines drawn freehand to form a series of boxes. The starting point on the rim is indicated by an upright line with heavy dots on it. The number of signs in a group varies from two to seven. In thirteen cases the sign at the left end of a group has an oblique stroke added underneath with a stylus.

The number of different signs is forty-five, but it must not be assumed that this is the total number of signs in the script, since a sample as short as this is unlikely to contain an example of every sign. Statistically it can be shown that the total 'population' of which this is a sample is likely to be at least fifty, and if there are more than a few very rare signs, the total may be sixty or more. This number, combined with the length of the groups of signs, makes it virtually certain that here too we are dealing with a simple syllabic system. The specimen does not appear to contain any ideograms or numerals, and this makes it hard to guess what sort of text it contains. This has allowed would-be decipherers, who are numerous, to propose the most implausible suggestions. The general tendency has been to assume it is some kind of religious text, which has the advantage of permitting the wildest flights of fancy.

The signs with a stroke underneath occur only at the ends of sign groups. This makes it likely that they are some kind of diacritical mark used to modify the reading of the sign to which they are attached. If the signs normally have the values of a consonant followed by a vowel, the strokes might be a means of cancelling the final vowel, so as to write a word ending in a consonant. No script of the Minoan family discussed in this book has such a device, but the *Devanagari* script used for Sanskrit has a similar mark which is used in this way.

It has been observed that a number of the longer sign groups begin with the same two signs. This might suggest that we are dealing with a language which uses prefixes rather than suffixes to modify the meaning of words. But there is a danger in putting much weight on this deduction without a great deal more evidence, for the same effect would be visible in such languages as Greek or French, if they too were written in a syllabic script. This is because the definite article is regularly treated as part of the following noun. Consider for instance the French series: *homme, l'homme, les hommes*. If these were written phonetically, it would appear that we had a word *om* to which the prefixes *l-* and *lez-* could be added.

If we had an adequate sample, such problems might be resolved, but we cannot even identify the type to which the language belongs, much less its linguistic family. We do not know the place of origin of the script, and as shown above there is a fair chance that it is not native to Crete, though this cannot be excluded. We have no means of guessing, even approximately, the nature of the text, for nothing like it has been found written in any known language.

All this could change if more specimens of the script were to be found. No script is in theory undecipherable, even if the language is totally unknown. But in order to make any progress it is essential to have enough texts, and these must be sufficiently variable, not merely repetitions of the same few formulas. Moreover, some of the inscriptions must be found in contexts which allow us to deduce approximately the meaning of some words without reference to their phonetic values. Only a large deposit of similar documents could open the way to a true decipherment of the Phaistos Disk.

This problem has not prevented enthusiastic amateurs all over the world from indulging in wild speculation. The problem is attractive precisely because it is so limited; it is the limitation which prevents certain deductions which also allows scope for misplaced ingenuity. A few decipherments have been proposed using known languages, including a few based upon Greek, despite the obvious improbability of such a solution at this date. What is worse, their authors are rarely aware of what Greek would look like at this period, at least four hundred years before Mycenaean.

But there is an even easier solution, which is to abandon the attempt to make the text fit a known language, and to invent a new language for the purpose. If you have a word which resembles something appropriate in Greek, you can give it that meaning. But if the next word is meaningless in Greek, you look for something suitable in Latin or Sanskrit or Persian, or whatever language takes your fancy. There is of course no way of proving such a language did not exist; there must have been thousands of languages once spoken, which are now totally forgotten. What is always overlooked is that if you abandon the rigour imposed by a known language, you destroy also any means of finding evidence to support your solution.

Others have failed to understand the conclusions to be drawn from the statistics, which establish the type of script, and have assumed that the signs, or some of them, are ideograms. It is then tempting to try to interpret them by looking for the object they represent, and give them values simply by inspection. The history of writing shows unmistakeably that values can hardly ever be guessed by this method. We cannot perhaps rule out the posssibility of a mixed system, part ideographic and part phonetic; but this would require a very large number of different signs, and thus the making of a large set of stamps to be able to write any but the simplest texts. There have even been decipherers who have proposed to regard it not as a script at all, but as some kind of tool or device, and one of my correspondents seriously suggested that it was really a chart for inter-planetary navigation. Science fiction has a lot to answer for.

My own view, shared by all serious scholars, is that the Disk is undecipherable so long as it remains an isolated document. Only a large increase in the number of inscriptions will permit real progress towards a decipherment. Meanwhile, we must curb our impatience, and admit that if King Minos himself were to reveal to someone in a dream the true interpretation, it would be quite impossible for him to convince anyone else that his was the one and only possible solution.

The Location of the Inscriptions

Specimens of most of the scripts mentioned in this book are to be seen in the Archaeological Museum of Iraklion, Crete. This holds the major collection of Linear B tablets from Knossos, most of the Linear A inscriptions, and the Phaistos Disk. The Linear B tablets from Pylos are all in the National Museum in Athens, together with some from Mycenae. A selection of these is on exhibition. There are small numbers of Linear B tablets in the Archaeological Museums of Thebes and Navplion.

The Ashmolean Museum, Oxford, has a collection of Linear B tablets from Knossos, donated by Evans while he was in charge of the Museum, and a few specimens of Linear A. The British Museum, London, has a few specimens of Linear B, and some classical Cypriot inscriptions. Isolated Linear B tablets are in Cambridge, Manchester and University College, London. Classical Cypriot inscriptions are also to be found in a number of Museums in western Europe.

All the more recent finds from Cyprus are of course still on the island, mostly at the Archaeological Museum in Nicosia. The Cypro–Minoan documents found at Ugarit (Ras Shamra) are in the National Museum of Damascus.

Bibliographical Note

There is now a vast bibliography of Linear B, but most of it is highly technical and to be found in learned journals. For English readers I should like to refer to my own two books, *The Decipherment of Linear B*, (2nd edn. Cambridge, 1967), and for the contents of the tablets, *The Mycenaean World* (Cambridge, 1976). For more advanced study, the major books in English are: Ventris, M. and Chadwick, J., *Documents in Mycenaean Greek* (2nd edn. Cambridge, 1973); and Palmer L. R., *The Interpretation of Mycenaean Greek Texts*, (Oxford, 1963). A useful study of decipherment is Barber, E. J. W., *Archaeological Decipherment*, (Princeton, 1974).

On Linear A and the various Cypriot scripts there is no satisfactory general publication in English. The Linear A texts have been collected and excellently edited by Godart, L. and Olivier, J-P., *Receuil des Inscriptions en Linéaire A*, 5 vols., Paris, 1976–85. The best collection of classical Cypriot inscriptions is Masson, O., *Les Inscriptions Chypriotes Syllabiques* (Paris, 1961). For the Phaistos Disk, there is an excellent photographic edition by Olivier, J-P., *Le Disque de Phaistos*, (École française d' Athènes, 1975), and a full discussion of the problems by Duhoux, Y., *Le Disque de Phaestos*, (Louvain, 1977).

Index